bxjc

Sports Illustrated KIDS

FANTASY BASEBALL MATH

USING STATS TO SCORE BIG IN YOUR LEAGUE

BY ALLAN MOREY

CAPSTONE PRESS
a capstone imprint

Sports Illustrated Kids Fantasy Sports Math is published by Capstone Press,
1710 Roe Crest Drive, North Mankato, Minnesota 56003.
www.mycapstone.com

Library of Congress Cataloging-in-Publication Data
Names: Morey, Allan.
Title: Fantasy baseball math : using stats to score big in your league / by Allan Morey.
Description: Mankato, Minnesota : Capstone Press, [2017] | Series: Sports Illustrated Kids.
   Fantasy Sports Math | Includes bibliographical references and index. | Audience: Ages: 8-12. |
   Audience: Grades: 4 to 6. | Description based on print version record and CIP data provided by
   publisher; resource not viewed.
Identifiers: LCCN 2015051398 (print) | LCCN 2015049424 (ebook) | ISBN 9781515721741 (eBook PDF) |
   ISBN 9781515721673 (library binding) | ISBN 9781515721703 (paperback)
Subjects: LCSH: Fantasy baseball (Game)—Mathematical models—Juvenile literature.
Classification: LCC GV1202.F33 (print) | LCC GV1202.F33 M47 2017 (ebook) | DDC 793.93001/5118—dc23
LC record available at http://lccn.loc.gov/2015051398

Summary: Describes how to use statistics and math to create and run a successful fantasy baseball team.

Editorial Credits
Aaron Sautter, editor; Sarah Bennett, designer; Eric Gohl, media researcher; Katy LaVigne, production specialist

Photo Credits
Getty Images: Christian Petersen, 8-9; Newscom: Cal Sport Media/John Mersits, 22, Icon Sportswire/Tony Ding,
21, Icon Sportswire/Warren Wimmer, 27, Icon Sportswire CBP/Russell Lansford, 18-19, Icon Sportswire DCT/
Frank Jansky, 24-25, Icon Sportswire DEK/Peter Llewellyn, 6-7, Icon Sportswire DEL/Ken Murray, 23, USA Today
Sports/Jeff Curry, 28-29, USA Today Sports/Peter Llewellyn, 4-5; Shutterstock: Freer, 2-3; Sports Illustrated: Al
Tielemans, 11, 14-15, 16-17, Damian Strohmeyer, 12, David E. Klutho, cover, Robert Beck, 20

Design Elements: Shutterstock

Printed and bound in the United States of America.
009678F16

TABLE OF CONTENTS

Rougned Odor

BATTER UP!

Major League Baseball (MLB) is an exciting game of home runs and strikeouts. But you don't need to be a big-hitting slugger or pitching ace to get in on the action. With fantasy baseball, you can feel the excitement of slamming a home run or zipping a fastball over the plate. Running your own all-star fantasy team helps bring your pro baseball dreams to life.

Baseball is a **statistics**-driven game. Everything is tracked, from a batter's hits to a pitcher's strikes thrown. Learning who the best players are can help you succeed. But you'll need to know more to dominate your league. You'll need to understand how players rack up their stats. You'll also want to know how each position can affect your team. With this knowledge, and some careful planning, you can capture the glory of a championship!

FANTASY FACT

In the 1970s baseball historian Bill James developed a new way of looking at baseball stats. He called it Sabermetrics. This system analyzes a player's stats to determine his ability to help his team.

statistics—numbers, facts, or other data collected about a specific subject

CHAPTER 1

UNDERSTANDING THE STATS

Fantasy baseball is a stat-driven game. The secret to a winning fantasy team is understanding how the stats work. There are a lot of player stats to track. But with practice you'll learn how various players can bring you success.

Batting Stats

Most batting stats are simple to understand. A player earns a run (R) for crossing home plate. He gets a home run (HR) for knocking one out of the park. But other batting stats are a bit trickier, such as runs batted in (RBI). A batter earns an RBI by helping a runner score, even if it's himself. When a batter hits a home run, he adds the home run, a run, and an RBI to his stats. One big blast can affect several batting stats!

There are also percentage-based stats like batting average (BA). This is the percentage of time a batter gets a hit when he's at the plate.

$$BA = Hits \div At\ Bats$$

If the Miami Marlins' Giancarlo Stanton has four at bats in a game and gets three hits, what is his batting average? Check your answer below.

FANTASY FACT

Barry Bonds set a record .609 on base percentage in 2004. He got on base more than 60 percent of the time. He was one of the most-feared power hitters at that time. Pitchers walked him a lot, which led to his scoring an incredible 129 runs that year.

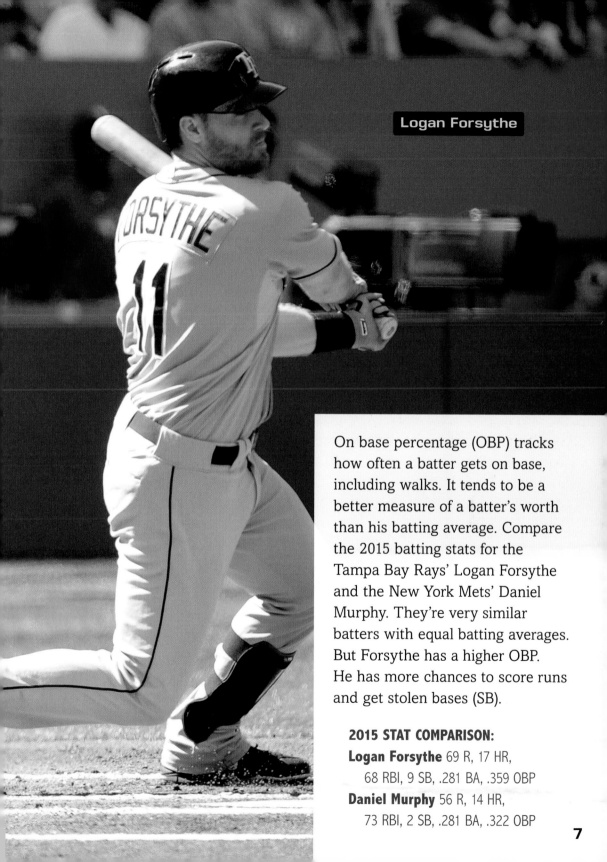

Logan Forsythe

On base percentage (OBP) tracks how often a batter gets on base, including walks. It tends to be a better measure of a batter's worth than his batting average. Compare the 2015 batting stats for the Tampa Bay Rays' Logan Forsythe and the New York Mets' Daniel Murphy. They're very similar batters with equal batting averages. But Forsythe has a higher OBP. He has more chances to score runs and get stolen bases (SB).

2015 STAT COMPARISON:
Logan Forsythe 69 R, 17 HR,
    68 RBI, 9 SB, .281 BA, .359 OBP
Daniel Murphy 56 R, 14 HR,
    73 RBI, 2 SB, .281 BA, .322 OBP

Zack Greinke

Pitching Stats

Pitching stats can be a little more complex than batting stats. Wins (W), strikeouts (SO), and saves (S) are simple enough. But a pitcher's **earned run** average (ERA) takes more effort to figure out.

A pitcher's ERA is an important measure of his value. The lower the number is, the better. It means the pitcher gives up few runs to the opposing team. To figure out a pitcher's ERA, first multiply the number of runs he gives up by nine. Then divide the result by the number of innings he actually pitched.

ERA = Earned Runs Allowed × 9 Innings Per Game ÷ Innings Pitched

If Arizona Diamondbacks pitcher Zack Greinke pitches seven innings and gives up two earned runs, what is his ERA? Check below to see if your answer is correct.

WHIP

WHIP is another common pitching stat. It stands for walks and hits allowed per inning pitched. WHIP measures how much control a pitcher has over the game. The fewer hits and walks he gives up, the fewer chances the opposing team has to score.

WHIP = (Walks + Hits) ÷ Innings Pitched

So if Zack Greinke gives up 5 hits and 1 walk in seven innings, what would be his WHIP? Do the math, then check below to see if you got it right.

earned run—a run scored by an opposing team that is not the result of a defensive error

CHAPTER 2

TYPES OF FANTASY LEAGUES

Your fantasy baseball team's goal is to rack up stats. But which are the most important, and how do they help you? It all depends on how your league is set up.

Understanding Categories

Most fantasy baseball leagues track stats with categories like home runs or strikeouts. Most leagues use eight or ten categories, which are divided equally between batting and pitching. For example, a 5 x 5 league uses 10 categories. It will have five batting and five pitching categories.

Head-to-Head Leagues

In a head-to-head (H2H) league, you face a new team during each **scoring period**. Your players' stats are totaled and then compared to your opponent's players. Each category you win counts as a win for your team. Each category you lose counts as a loss. There can even be ties.

FANTASY FACT

Instead of categories, some leagues use a point system. Each stat used is given a point value. For example, hitting a double is worth 2 points while earning a save is worth 5. The team with the most points at the end of a scoring period earns the win.

scoring period—the length of time that stats are totaled in a head-to-head match; in most H2H leagues, scoring periods last one week

Look at the two teams in the chart below. They play in a 5 x 5 H2H league. Each team competes in 10 categories. What is the win-loss record for the Brickhouse Bombers? Hint: for ERA and WHIP, lower numbers are better. Find the answer below.

TEAM	R	HR	RBI	SB	BA	W	SO	S	ERA	WHIP
Brickhouse Bombers	29	7	32	4	.285	3	42	7	3.45	1.26
Home Run Kids	22	4	25	9	.309	5	56	7	2.97	1.14

After every scoring period, a team's wins, losses, and ties are added to its overall record. Then at the end of the season, the best teams battle in the playoffs for the championship.

FANTASY POINT *EXPLOSION*

Max Scherzer SP, Washington Nationals (vs NY Mets) October 3, 2015

1 W, 17 K, 0 S, 0.00 ERA, 0.00 WHIP

Answer: 3–6–1; 3 Wins (runs, home runs, runs batted in), 6 Losses (stolen bases, batting average, wins, strikeouts, ERA, WHIP), and 1 Tie (saves).

11

Roto Leagues

Diehard fantasy fans rave about rotisserie, or roto, leagues. They argue that stat totals, not win-loss records, show who has the best team. In roto leagues stats are added up over the course of an entire season to earn points. Then at the end of the season, the team with the most points wins the championship.

Check out following grid for a 10-team, 4 x 4 roto league. Each team is ranked 1-10 in each category. The higher a team's ranking, the more points it gets. For example, the Juggling Judsters have the most home runs with 112. They score 10 points in that category. Meanwhile, the Prince Fielders have the fewest home runs with 71. They score just 1 point.

FANTASY POINT *EXPLOSION*

Edwin Encarnación 1B, Toronto Blue Jays
(vs Detroit Tigers) August 29, 2015

4 R, 3 HR, 9 RBI, 0 SB, .600 BA

Winning categories can help your team score points. But doing great in some categories and poorly in others won't necessarily win you a championship. The goal is to do well across the board. The Monster Mashers are winning the most categories with three: stolen bases, wins, and strikeouts. They scored 52 total points. But the team didn't win the title. Which team actually takes home the trophy? (Hint: for ERA, the lowest number scores the most points.) Check below for the correct answer.

(X) = points scored for each category

TEAM NAME	HR	RBI	SB	BA	W	SO	S	ERA	TOTAL POINTS
Fastballers	87 (4)	527 (3)	39 (6)	.296 (8)	32 (8)	376 (8)	24 (6)	3.26 (6)	49
Brickhouse Bombers	102 (7)	545 (5)	52 (9)	.286 (4)	25 (4)	362 (5)	15 (2)	3.45 (4)	40
Home Run Kids	84 (3)	489 (1)	42 (7)	.288 (5)	29 (6)	369 (7)	12 (1)	2.96 (8)	38
Prince Fielders	71 (1)	570 (7)	38 (5)	.293 (6)	18 (1)	298 (1)	29 (9)	3.12 (7)	37
Jackhammering Jacks	110 (9)	612 (10)	26 (3)	.279 (2)	31 (7)	341 (3)	26 (8)	2.76 (10)	52
Juggling Judsters	112 (10)	539 (4)	15 (1)	.275 (1)	19 (2)	326 (2)	17 (3)	4.21 (1)	24
Knuckleballers	98 (6)	569 (6)	47 (8)	.307 (10)	28 (5)	363 (6)	25 (7)	2.82 (9)	57
The Mousers	104 (8)	576 (8)	18 (2)	.294 (7)	36 (9)	406 (9)	32 (10)	3.78 (3)	56
Monster Mashers	95 (5)	514 (2)	68 (10)	.302 (9)	38 (10)	412 (10)	18 (4)	3.87 (2)	52
The Terrible Tys	79 (2)	581 (9)	31 (4)	.284 (3)	20 (3)	346 (4)	20 (5)	3.35 (5)	35

FANTASY FACT

Sportswriter and editor Dan Okrent created rotisserie fantasy baseball in the early 1980s. He and his friends started it as a way to show off their knowledge of pro baseball.

Answer: The Knuckleballers win with 57 total points.

CHAPTER 3

PLAYER POSITIONS

After stats and categories, you need to consider **roster** size and player positions. MLB teams have 25-player rosters. Fantasy teams often use the same number of players. Fantasy baseball also includes the same positions as the pros. That means you'll need at least eight batters in your **starting lineup**.

1 Catcher (C)

1 First Baseman (1B)

1 Second Baseman (2B)

1 Third Baseman (3B)

1 Shortstop (SS)

3 Outfielders (OF)

Sluggers vs. Speedsters

Power hitters often rack up more home runs and RBIs. Meanwhile, speedy second basemen and shortstops tend to get more stolen bases. Look at the below 2015 stats for the Los Angeles Angels' Albert Pujols and Miami Marlins' Dee Gordon. How does a first baseman slugger compare to a speedy second baseman? Both are strong in certain categories. Which do you think adds more value to your team?

2015 STAT COMPARISON:

Albert Pujols (1B): 85 R, 40 HR, 95 RBI, 5 SB, .244 BA

Dee Gordon (2B): 88 R, 4 HR, 46 RBI, 58 SB, .333 BA

roster—a list of players on a team

starting lineup—the players whose stats are counted during a scoring period

Starling Marté

FANTASY FACT

There is one big difference between the American League (AL) and the National League (NL). The NL makes pitchers bat. The AL uses a designated hitter (DH) instead. If your league uses the DH, it could mean adding one more batter to your starting lineup.

5-Tool Players

One type of player can be especially valuable to your fantasy team. These players are known as 5-tool players, such as Pittsburgh Pirates outfielder Starling Marté. Unlike Pujols and Gordon, Marté can help your team in all five categories. If you can get one or more of these players on your team, you'll be in great shape.

2015 STAT COMPARISON:
Starling Marté (OF): 84 R, 19 HR, 81 RBI, 30 SB, .287 BA

Francisco Rodriguez

Pitchers

In fantasy baseball, pitchers are just as important as batters for your team's success. Pitchers can rack up numbers that may put your team over the top. Most fantasy leagues use the same number of batters as pitchers. So if you have eight batters in your starting lineup, you'll also have eight pitchers. Here's a typical breakdown used by many teams:

5 Starting Pitchers (SP)   3 Relief Pitchers (RP)

Starters vs. Relievers

The number of innings a player pitches can greatly affect his stats. Starters work more innings than relievers, so they're usually more valuable. Check out the stat lines below for two top pitchers. The Washington Nationals' Max Scherzer pitched 228 2/3 innings in 2015. Meanwhile, Francisco Rodriguez pitched only 57 innings for the Milwaukee Brewers. Which pitcher do you think is more valuable for your team? Check below to see if you picked the better player.

2015 STAT COMPARISON:
Max Scherzer (SP): 14 W, 2.79 ERA, 0 S, 276 SO, 0.92 WHIP
Francisco Rodriguez (RP): 1 W, 2.21 ERA, 38 S, 62 SO, 0.86 WHIP

TYPES OF RELIEVERS

There are two types of relief pitchers to keep in mind. **Closers** tend to be more valuable than middle relievers. They can rack up saves, which can be a valuable fantasy stat. But strong middle relievers can be handy too. Arizona Cardinals pitcher Kevin Siegrist was one of the best relievers in 2015. Check how his stats compare to ace closer Francisco Rodriguez above.

Kevin Siegrist (RP): 7 W, 2.17 ERA, 6 S, 90 SO, 1.17 WHIP

Siegrist has a slight edge in three out of five categories. He also earned a handful of saves. He's considered a 5-tool pitcher who can be a big help for a fantasy team.

Answer: Scherzer is the better player to own, with more wins and strikeouts. As a starting pitcher, he has more chances to pump up his stats.

closer—the pitcher who throws the final out of a game

CHAPTER 4

THE DRAFT

You've learned about stats and categories. You know about player positions and how leagues work. Now comes the fun part. It's time for the **draft**! Picking players is where you begin to build a winning team.

The Snake Draft

Most leagues use a snake draft to pick players. The picking order is reversed for each round. The team picking first in one round picks last in the next. This format helps even out the odds of getting good players.

Check out the following draft order chart. Team 1 gets to pick the league's best player in Round 1. But in Round 2 they drop down to pick number 20. It's hard to know if any top players will still be available. On the other hand, Team 10 gets to pick back-to-back with picks 10 and 11. They're guaranteed to get two star players.

ROUND	TEAM 1	TEAM 2	TEAM 3	TEAM 4	TEAM 5	TEAM 6	TEAM 7	TEAM 8	TEAM 9	TEAM 10
1	Pick 1	Pick 2	Pick 3	Pick 4	Pick 5	Pick 6	Pick 7	Pick 8	Pick 9	Pick 10
2	Pick 20	Pick 19	Pick 18	Pick 17	Pick 16	Pick 15	Pick 14	Pick 13	Pick 12	Pick 11

draft—the process of choosing players for a team

A.J. Pollock OF, Arizona Diamondbacks
(vs Cincinnati Reds) August 21, 2015

3 R, 1 HR, 1 RBI, 2 SB, .800 BA

A.J. Pollock

Auction Drafts

In auction drafts, a league uses a salary cap. This is the maximum amount of fantasy money a team can spend on its roster. Instead of picking players, team owners take turns bidding on them. The owner bidding the most money gets the player.

Say you have $200 to spend on a 25-player roster. You've already won the bidding on the following players.

Mike Trout

Mike Trout (OF), Los Angeles Angels $32
David Price (SP), Boston Red Sox $20
Robinson Canó (2B), Seattle Mariners $16

Auctions can be tricky. In this example, you spent $68 to get some great players. But you still have 22 slots left to fill. You have to be careful not to spend too much too early in the draft. If you spend a lot on a few stars, you may have to fill your roster with low quality players. You have $132 left. What is the average amount you can spend on the rest of your players? Check your answer on the next page. You may be able to fill your roster. But the quality of your players will likely be iffy at best.

Check your answer on the next page.

FANTASY FACT

Some leagues limit the available player pool. There might be a rule saying that only American League or only National League players can be selected.

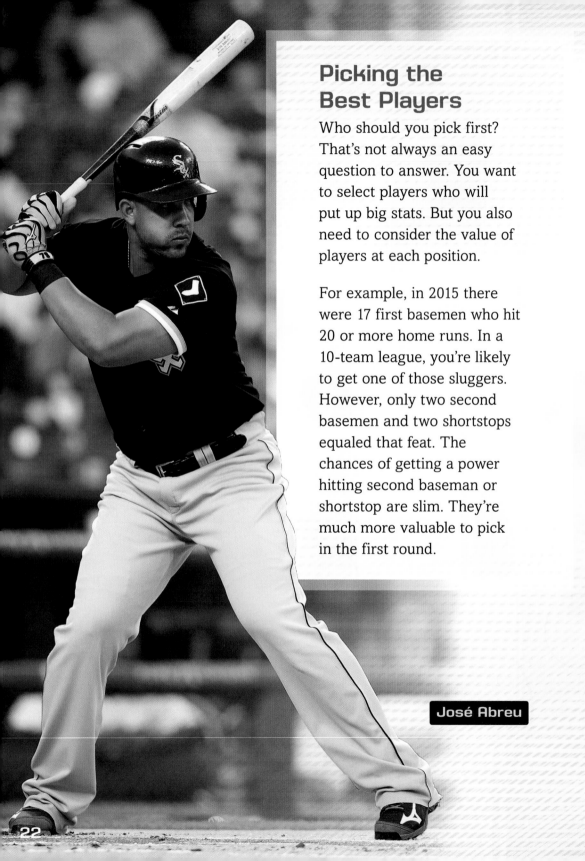

Picking the Best Players

Who should you pick first? That's not always an easy question to answer. You want to select players who will put up big stats. But you also need to consider the value of players at each position.

For example, in 2015 there were 17 first basemen who hit 20 or more home runs. In a 10-team league, you're likely to get one of those sluggers. However, only two second basemen and two shortstops equaled that feat. The chances of getting a power hitting second baseman or shortstop are slim. They're much more valuable to pick in the first round.

José Abreu

Compare the following two scenarios. Add up the stats for each pair of batters in each category. Then compare the totals. Which set of players wins more categories? Check your answer below.

Drafting a top slugging 2B and then a good 1B.
Round 1: Brian Dozier, Minnesota Twins (2B): 101 R, 28 HRs, 77 RBI, 12 SB
Round 2: José Abreu, Chicago White Sox (1B): 88 R, 30 HR, 101 RBI, 0 SB

Drafting a top slugging 1B and then a good 2B.
Round 1: Edwin Encarnación, Toronto Blue Jays (1B): 94 R, 39 HR, 111 RBI, 3 SB
Round 2: Rougned Odor, Texas Rangers (2B): 54 R, 16 HR, 61 RBI, 6 SB

Dallas Keuchel

SLUGGERS BEFORE HURLERS

Batters tend to put up more consistent stats than pitchers from year to year. The Houston Astros' Dallas Keuchel was one of the top pitchers in 2015. But check his stats over a three-year span. What are his average wins per year?

2015 – 20 W, 2.48 ERA, 0 S, 216 SO, 1.02 WHIP
2014 – 12 W, 2.93 ERA, 0 S, 146 SO, 1.18 WHIP
2013 – 6 W, 5.15 ERA, 0 S, 124 SO, 1.54 WHIP

Keuchel's three-year win average is just 12.7. He could be a risky pick early in a draft. You don't know if he'll have another 20-win season or play closer to his average. However, New York Mets slugger Yoenis Céspedes averaged a solid 27 home runs over that same span. He would be a safer bet to produce big numbers for your team.

Answers:
Dozier and Abreu win 4–0. They offer the best value for your team.

CHAPTER 5

MANAGING YOUR TEAM

You have your roster. But you can't relax. Your job as a fantasy baseball owner is just beginning. To achieve fantasy glory, you'll need to manage your team throughout the season. Players might get injured and need to be replaced. Or you may need to switch out a player to make your team stronger.

Multiple Starts

Fantasy owners will always want to start their stars. But for average players, you'll want to consider how often they actually play. A typical scoring period is one week. MLB teams play five to seven games a week. Most teams start five pitchers on a five-day rotation. During a scoring period, you may be lucky and have one or two pitchers take the mound twice to rack up stats.

However, if you had to start just one of the following pitchers, you'd normally give the Chicago Cubs' Jake Arrieta the nod. He has much better overall stats. But what if Cleveland Indians hurler Danny Salazar gets two starts in a scoring period while Arrieta gets only one?

Jake Arrieta: 22 W 1.77 ERA, 236 SO, 0 S, 0.87 WHIP
Danny Salazar: 14 W, 3.45 ERA, 195 SO, 0 S, 1.13 WHIP

Arrieta has a much better ERA. But with two starts, Salazar could get more wins and strikeouts. He would likely be the better starter for that scoring period.

Danny Salazar

The number of games played is also important for batters. Say you have a good batter playing in five games and an average batter playing in seven. Which should you put in your starting lineup for the week? The average player will have more chances to put up stats for your team. So he may be the better choice.

Roster Changes

Sometimes players don't live up to expectations. And sometimes they may get hurt. In these cases you'll need to look at adding **free agents** or making a **trade**.

The easiest way to improve your roster is by picking up free agents. But don't be tempted to drop a good player who's in a slump just to add an average player who's hot. You could get burned. Take Philadelphia Phillies third baseman Maikel Franco for example. Compare his June 2015 stats to his year-end totals.

> **June stats:** 18 R, 8 HR, 24 RBI, 0 SB, .352 BA
>
> **Year-end stats:** 45 R, 14 HR, 50 RBI, 1 SB, .280 BA

Franco tore it up in June. But that one hot month could fool you. How many runs, home runs, and RBIs did he average for the other five months of the season? Subtract the June stats from the year-end totals, and then divide by five. Check your answers on the next page.

Trades

Making trades with another team can be useful, but it can also be tricky. The goal with trading is to improve your team while not giving away players you need. Look at your team's strengths. If you have two solid shortstops, you could consider trading one of them. Find a team that's weak at that position and offer to make a trade. Compare the stats of the player you're offering to the one you want. You want to make sure you're getting good value for the player you're giving up. But don't be discouraged if your offer is rejected. Every owner is looking to improve his or her team. Some owners are just more willing to trade than others.

FANTASY FACT

Some fantasy leagues may also use a disabled list (DL). These are slots used for stashing injured players. If one of your players goes down, you can put him on the DL. Then you'll have an open slot to fill with a free agent.

free agent—a player who is not on another team

trade—an agreement between two or more teams to exchange players

← Maikel Franco

Answer: 5.4 R, 1.2 HR, and 5.2 RBIs. Take out June's numbers, and Franco probably isn't someone to add to your team.

27

Capturing the Trophy

You may never smash a grand slam home run. You might not be able to pitch a shutout game. But with fantasy baseball you can still taste the excitement of being in the big leagues. Fantasy baseball is more than just a game of numbers and stats. It's a way to get in on the action and root for your favorite players. It's also a great way to hang out with friends and talk about your favorite pastime.

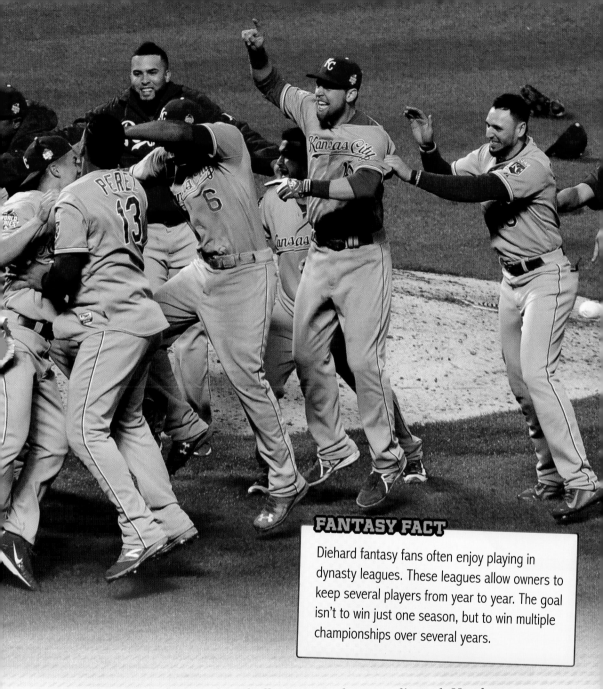

Running a fantasy baseball team can be complicated. You have to manage multiple offensive and defensive players. There are also tons of stats to track and analyze to get an edge. But with a little math knowledge and practice, you'll soon understand player stats and how they can work to your advantage. Before long you'll be the proud owner of a championship team and hoisting your league's fantasy trophy.

GLOSSARY

closer (KLOHZ-uhr)—the pitcher who throws the final out of a game

draft (DRAFT)—the process of choosing players for a team

earned run (URND RUN)—a run scored by an opposing team that is not the result of a defensive error

free agent (FREE AYJ-uhnt)—a player who is not on another team

roster (ROS-tur)—a list of players on a team

scoring period (SKOR-ing PEER-ee-uhd)—the length of time that stats are totaled in a head-to-head match; in most H2H leagues, scoring periods last one week

starting lineup (STAR-ting LYN-uhp)—the players whose stats are counted during a scoring period

statistics (stuh-TISS-tiks)—numbers, facts, or other data collected about a specific subject

trade (TRAYD)—an agreement between two or more teams to exchange players

READ MORE

Braun, Eric. *Baseball Stats and the Stories Behind Them: What Every Fan Needs to Know.* Sports Stats and Stories. North Mankato, Minn.: Capstone Press, 2016.

Kortemeier, Todd. *Pro Baseball by the Numbers.* Pro Sports by the Numbers. North Mankato, Minn.: Capstone Press, 2016.

Murray, Stuart A. P. *Score with Baseball Math.* Score with Sports Math. Berkeley Heights, N.J.: Enslow Publishers, 2014.

INTERNET SITES

FactHound offers a safe, fun way to find Internet sites related to this book. All of the sites on FactHound have been researched by our staff.

Here's all you do:

Visit *www.facthound.com*

Type in this code: 9781515721673

 Check out projects, games and lots more at
www.capstonekids.com

INDEX